**WRITE YOUR OWN
STUPID MESSAGE.**

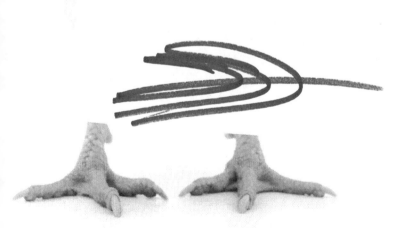

DAVID L. SLOAN

PHANTOM PRESS
K E Y W E S T

Editorial services: DorothyDrennen.com

Inquiries: david@phantompress.com

ISBN: 978-0-9789921-7-0

DEDICATED
TO
HOWARD STERN
&
KERRY PARKHOUSE SHUMAKER

NO ANIMALS WERE HARMED IN THE MAKING OF THIS BOOK.

**A PORTION OF THE AUTHORS PROCEEDS ARE
DONATED TO BIRD RESCUE ORGANIZATIONS.**

IT SHOULD
BE DEDICATED
TO ME.

ASSHOLE

ROOSTERS ARE ASSHOLES

IT
SHOULD
COME
AS
NO
SURPRISE
TO
YOU
THAT
ROOSTERS
ARE
ASSHOLES.

AN ASSHOLE ROOSTER CHASES ME AROUND THE FARM ALL DAY.

AN ASSHOLE ROOSTER
EATS MY KIBBLE AND
MAKES MY TUMMY
GROWL LIKE A BEAR.

A ROOSTER TRIED
TO HAVE SEX WITH MY WIFE.

IT IS SAFE TO SAY
ROOSTERS ARE ASSHOLES.

**THE FIRST KNOWN
ROOSTERS WERE A PAIR
OF COCKS SPOTTED
FIGHTING ON THE SIDE OF
THE ROAD IN GREECE BY
GENERAL THEMISTOCLES
IN THE 5TH CENTURY B.C.**

**THEMI HAD A SOFT SPOT
FOR COCKS, SO HE TOOK
THEM HOME TO BREED.**

THAT NIGHT
THEY ATE THE
TIP OF HIS FINGER.

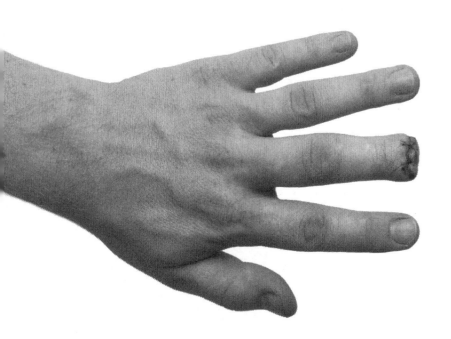

BECAUSE ROOSTERS ARE ASSHOLES.

YOU PROBABLY HATE
ROOSTERS WHEN
THEY WAKE YOU UP
IN THE MORNING
WITH THEIR
COCK-A-DOODLE-DOOING.

BUT AS FAR AS ROOSTERS
BEING ASSHOLES GOES...
THAT BARELY QUALIFIES AS
AN ASSHOLE MANEUVER

ROOSTERS INTENTIONALLY POOP ON THE PATH WHERE YOU INTEND TO WALK.

THEN THEY HIDE
IN NEARBY BUSHES
WITH THEIR FRIENDS
AND WAIT.

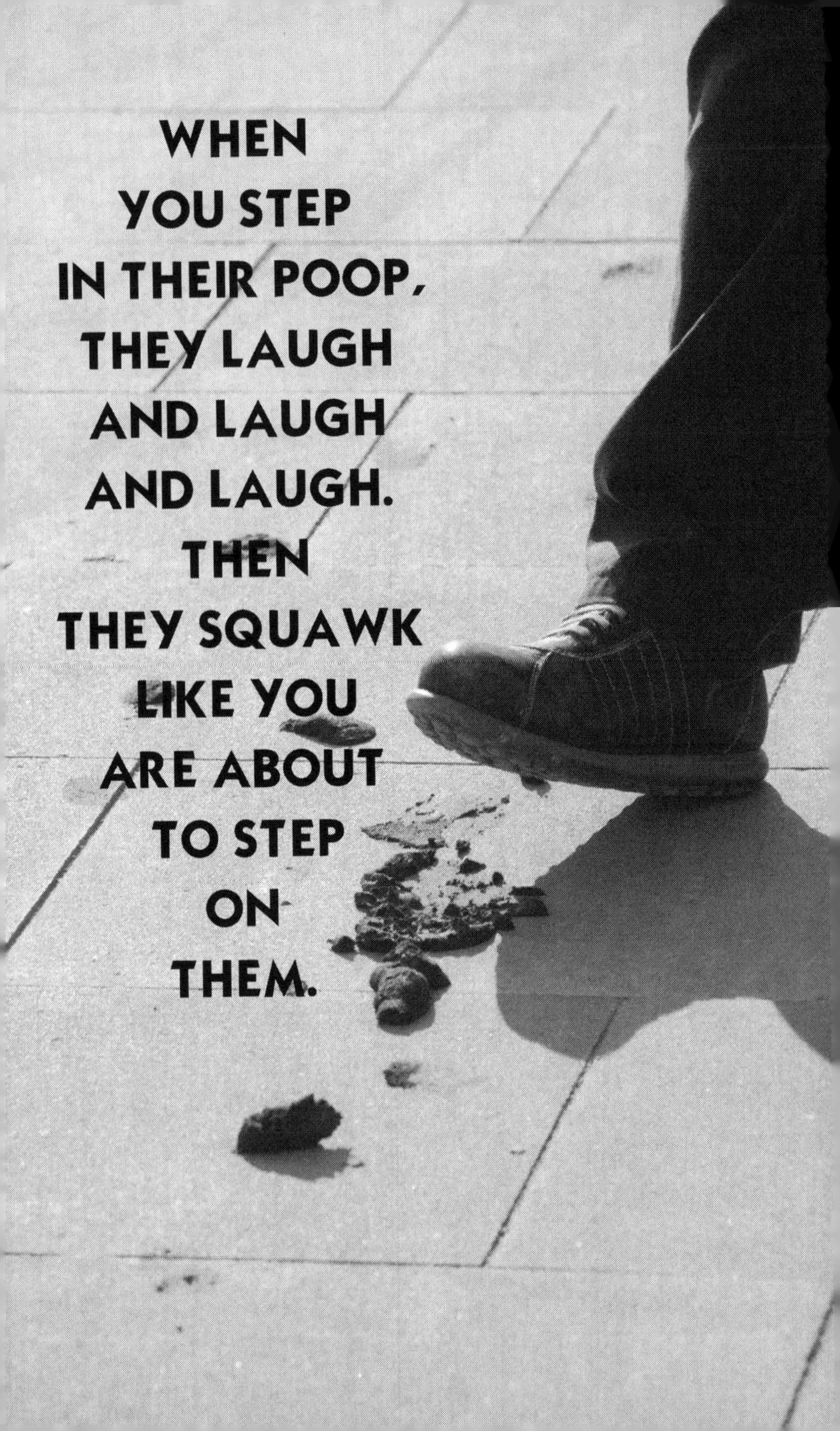

WHEN
YOU STEP
IN THEIR POOP,
THEY LAUGH
AND LAUGH
AND LAUGH.
THEN
THEY SQUAWK
LIKE YOU
ARE ABOUT
TO STEP
ON
THEM.

ROOSTERS
ARE
ASSHOLES!

MORE THAN
89%
OF RESTAURANTS
IN THE
UNITED STATES
FEATURE
CHICKEN
ON THEIR
MENUS.
LESS THAN
2%
FEATURE
ROOSTER.

MANY OF
THESE CHICKENS
ACTUALLY
ARE ROOSTERS,
BUT RESTAURANTS
DON'T WANT TO
REMIND YOU
THAT YOU
ARE
EATING
AN ASSHOLE

**ARCHEOLOGISTS BELIEVE
THAT ROOSTERS WERE
ORIGINALLY DOMESTICATED
- NOT TO EAT -
BUT
TO FIGHT.**

A
YOUNG
EASTERN EUROPEAN GIRL
NAMED MARIE
WAS THE FIRST TO TURN
THE ROOSTER
INTO
FOOD.

ACCORDING
TO LEGEND,
TWO ROOSTERS
STARTED FIGHTING
IN HER KITCHEN
AND KNOCKED A GLASS
OF WATER
ONTO HER CAT,

**MARIE
DRIED OFF HER CAT,
PUNCHED
EACH ROOSTER IN THE
FACE, AND HID
THEIR DEAD BODIES
IN A NEARBY
PIE.**

HER HUSBAND
CAME HOME,
ATE THE PIE,
AND LOVED IT.
AND THAT IS WHY
WE EAT ROOSTERS IN PIES
TO THIS DAY.

DID YOU KNOW ROOSTERS ARE RESPONSIBLE FOR 78% OF ALL BARNYARD CRIMES?

IF YOU WERE A ROOSTER COP YOU COULD PUT A STOP TO ALL OF THIS ROOSTER NONSENSE.

JUST PICTURE YOURSELF PULLING UP NEXT TO THOSE MOTHERCLUCKERS AND SAYING...

THE ROOSTERS WOULD IGNORE YOU.

OR LAUGH AT YOU.

OR THREATEN TO TAKE YOUR BADGE.

BUT
FINGERPRINTING
A ROOSTER
IS IMPOSSIBLE
ANYWAY,
SO JUST
PRETEND YOU
ARRESTED THE
MOST WANTED
ASSHOLE ROOSTERS
IN THE WORLD.

DAMN,
YOU
ARE GOOD.

COCK-A-DOODLE DREW

EXCESSIVE CROWING

Cock-a-doodle Drew, AKA 'that motherfucker crowing outside my window' was arrested with six neighborhood roosters as he demonstrated a technique for making the rooster call more annoying to the human ear. The roosters had a crudely drawn map of the neighborhood with grains of corn marking areas of optimal acoustic transmission. When asked how he evaded capture for so long, Cock-a-doodle Drew said it was just dumb cluck.

HARRY THE HAMMER

DISTURBING THE PEACE

Harry the Hammer was often referred to as a big dick for his practice of hypnotizing business people and forcing them to use his magic hammer against their own co-workers. He would gleefully ride the magic hammer as it pounded the surprised movers and shakers into the ground past their waists without doing any damage to their heads. It is suspected that he did not wield the hammer himself because he was chicken. His bail has been set at $26.

TIM

PUBLIC NUISANCE

There once was a rooster who left his farm in Kansas and hitchhiked his way across the great country of America so he could see the majestic ocean that all of the local trout talked about. When he made it to the beach in Florida he saw a sea turtle nest, forgot all about the ocean and started crushing the sea turtle eggs with his gangly feet. This Rooster did not give a damn about sea turtle babies because he was an asshole. When the arresting officer asked for identification, he indicated that some people called him Tim.

TUXEDO PETE

IMPERSONATING A PENGUIN

Tuxedo Pete Partridge was detained at a Texas zoo after the head zookeeper spotted a pool of blood in the penguin enclosure. A review of the live penguin cam revealed that Pete entered the enclosure wearing a penguin suit. Unable to maintain his balance on the ice, he slid into one of the real penguins, causing lacerations across her tummy with his sharp rooster claws. The penguin is expected to make a full recovery. A newspaper article described the scene as "black and white and red all over." Tuxedo Pete is an asshole.

STICKY CLAW STEVE

GRAND THEFT AUTO

Sticky Claw Steve was arrested after leading cops on a wild goose chase down Main Street in a stolen pink and green Miata belonging to a popular local grain farmer. Though the exterior of the Miata was not damaged, the interior seat had several scratch marks. Beak marks were noticed on the steering wheel, gas pedal and clutch. While being detained, Sticky Claw Steve was overheard saying that only pussies drive Miatas.

SIDNEY THE SNEAK

UNAUTHORIZED FERTILIZATION

Sidney the Sneak has been brought to justice after the baby chick population in Springfield more than tripled over a four-month period, much to the annoyance of local egg farmers. In the months leading up to the population boom, local farmers had reported suspicious sounds coming from their hen houses that they attributed to a local fox. Originally confused as to how a fox would mate with a hen, they now believe the noises were coming from Mr. Sneak.

JACKKNIFE JOHNNY

CONSPIRACY TO KILL HUMANS

Jackknife Johnny was a floor mopping flunky and tool of the dagger's drawn world. He was apprehended washing cars down in Dallas after vendors at a local farm market found yellow Post-it notes attached to their produce promising a slow and painful death. The notes were not stuck to the produce, but were affixed with bloody jackknives stolen from a nearby jackknife store. Johnny was strung out on morphine and meth at the time of his arrest.

BENNY THE BOMBER

ASSHOLE BUSTED

NUCLEAR THREAT AHEAD

HARBORING WEAPONS OF MASS DESTRUCTION

Adding more proof that roosters are assholes, Benny the Bomber was arrested this week on suspicion of harboring weapons of mass destruction. It was discovered he had been operating a nuclear grenade scheme in which dangerous nuclear grenades were painted to look like eggs and smuggled to terrorist sleeper cells across the nation on the vehicles of unknowing egg-truck drivers. Members of Homeland Security were credited with cracking the case.

WHISKEY DICK

ASSHOLE BUSTED

DRUNK DRIVING

An alcoholic rooster known on the streets as Whiskey Dick turned himself in after encouraging yet another bar patron to drive him back to his tree despite the fact that they were visibly drunk and unfit to operate machinery. More than 200 drunk driving incidents have been attributed to Whiskey Dick. Upon turning himself in he stated he had lived a hard life and just couldn't keep it up anymore.

RANDOM PUPPY IN A SUITCASE

SID THE SCRAMBLER

ASSHOLE BUSTED

DOMESTIC VIOLENCE

What kind of chicken would spend several passionate nights in a hen house and return days later to peck, crack, stomp and destroy the very eggs he helped create? An asshole rooster named Sid the Scrambler. That's what kind. Look at those poor little eggs and how frightened they are. Thankfully there are good rooster cops like you to keep these unsavory fowl off the streets. The eggs were given a victims rights pamphlet.

BRADLEY THE BEAK

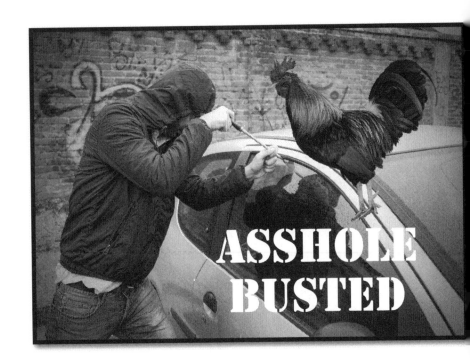

BEAKING AND ENTERING

Bradley the Beak brought crime to new levels in Maryville, TN after thieves realized that the shape, texture and durability of his beak made it the perfect tool for breaking into homes, businesses, vehicles, and even real estate lock boxes. The popularity of his technique led to the term 'beaking and entering.' The accompanying hash tag was trending on twitter for several days last fall. When asked to give up his accomplices, The Beak remained tightlipped.

CARL THE CLAW

COCK FIGHTING

Local authorities apprehended a rooster known in the cock fighting circuit as Carl the Claw (because his name was Carl and he used his claws to fight). No other information was available at press time, but it is assumed that all of the fighters were assholes to a degree.

WHAM BAM SAM

INTERSPECIES RELATIONS

The animal kingdom can breathe a sigh of relief now that the rooster they called Wham Bam Thank You Mam Sam is behind bars. Mr. Bam Thank You Mam Sam is accused of using an animal tranquilizer called ketamine to entice animals of different species into his pile of hay for a roll. He was arrested in the company of a confused donkey, a disoriented doggy and a slutty cat. Photographs found at the scene were confiscated by an investigator who had a creepy smile.

THE DIRTY DOZEN

STILL AT LARGE

Always be diligent in your travels. There are more roosters around every corner just waiting for an opportunity to be assholes.

THOSE ROOSTERS HAVE YOU PRETTY HEATED NOW, EH?

ウーロン茶

CALM YOURSELF DOWN BY WRITING A HAIKU.

DO NOT WORRY,
NOBODY REMEMBERS
HOW TO WRITE A HAIKU.

DEMENTIA

5 SYLLABLES
7 SYLLLABLES
5 SYLLABLES

Roses are red,
violets are blue,
if the truth be known,
I can't stand you.

**BUT YOU CAN
WRITE A POEM OR
A FREESTYLE RAP INSTEAD.**

IF YOU ARE
READING
THIS BOOK IN
THE BATHROOM,
PEOPLE
ARE PROBABLY
STARTING TO
WONDER WHERE
YOU ARE,
SO TRY TO
WRAP THINGS UP.

UNLESS YOU LIVE ALONE. IF YOU LIVE ALONE, TAKE YOUR TIME AND ENJOY THESE FASCINATING FACTS ABOUT ROOSTERS.

EGYPTIANS
HUNG ROOSTER
EGGS
IN TEMPLES
TO ENCOURAGE
THEIR RIVERS
TO FLOOD.

ACTUALLY, THEY WERE HEN
EGGS, BUT THIS IS A BOOK
ABOUT ROOSTERS SO JUST LET
IT SLIDE.

THE ROOSTER
IS ALSO A
SIGN OF VIRILITY,
SO FEEL FREE
TO JUMP IN WITH
YOUR OWN COCK
JOKE HERE IF YOU
HAVE NOT DONE
SO YET.

ZOROASTRIANS
BELIEVED ROOSTERS
CROWED AT DAWN
BECAUSE THEY WERE
POSSESSED BY SPIRITS
STRUGGLING BETWEEN
DARKNESS AND LIGHT.

I HAVE GHOST FEET.

GHOSTS

OOOOO.
HAUNTED ASSHOLES.

**ROMANS USED THE
ROOSTER TO PREDICT
HOW THEY WOULD
DO IN BATTLE.
A HUNGRY ROOSTER
INDICATED
THEY WOULD
WIN.**

IF THE ROOSTER PREDICTED
DOOM, THE ROMANS
WOULD KILL HIM.

BECAUSE ROMANS WERE
ASSHOLES TOO.

DID YOU KNOW
THE ORIGINAL LYRICS
TO LOUIE LOUIE
INCLUDED THE LINE
ROOSTERS ARE ASSHOLES?

IT IS PRETTY AMAZING
THAT YOU ARE
STILL READING THIS.
IT IS REALLY ONE OF
THOSE BOOKS A
FRIEND BUYS YOU
BECAUSE THEY KNOW
YOU HATE ROOSTERS
AND IT HAS A
CATCHY TITLE THAT
STATES HOW
YOU FEEL.

WE RAN OUT OF THINGS TO SAY 59 PAGES AGO

BUT AS LONG AS YOU ARE STILL HERE, HOW ABOUT A JOKE?

WHAT DID
THE ROOSTER
SAY TO THE
ONE-LEGGED FARMER?

NOTHING.
ANIMALS CANT TALK.

WHY DID
THE ROOSTER
GO TO KFC?

BECAUSE
HE WANTED TO
SEE A CHICKEN STRIP.

WHY DID THE ROOSTER PUSH THE CAT INTO THE RIVER?

BECAUSE ROOSTERS ARE ASSHOLES.

**WHAT DO YOU CALL A
ROOSTER WHO WAKES YOU
UP AT THE SAME TIME
EVERY MORNING?**

ASSHOLE

69

HOW MANY ROOSTERS
CAN YOU FIT
IN A BATH TUB?

IT DOESNT MATTER.
ROOSTERS ARE ASSHOLES.

A ROOSTER TAKES ABOUT 18-20 BREATHS PER MINUTE BUT HIS HEART BEATS ABOUT 300 TIMES IN THAT VERY SAME MINUTE.

ROOSTER SPERM CAN SURVIVE IN A HEN FOR UP TO 32 DISGUSTING DAYS.

ROOSTERS
HAVE
BEEN
KNOWN
TO
EAT
THEIR
BABIES
TOO.

TOTAL
ASSHOLES.

**THE ROOSTER
WAS ONCE A SACRED
ANIMAL SYMBOLIZING
THE SUN.**

**TODAY IT IS JUST
AN ASSHOLE.**

THERE
IS
ONE
ROOSTER
WHO
WAS
NOT
A
TOTAL
ASSHOLE.

THEY
CALLED
HIM
MIRACLE
MIKE.

A FARMER CUT HIS HEAD OFF IN 1945, BUT MIKE DID NOT DIE.

SO THE FARMER
AND HIS FAMILY
KEPT MIKE ALIVE FOR
18 MONTHS
BY FEEDING HIS
THROAT HOLE
WITH AN
EYE DROPPER.

THEY TRAVELED
THE STATE FAIR CIRCUIT
TOGETHER AND
THE FARMER
SHOWED OFF
THE DRIED,
SEVERED ROOSTER HEAD
UNTIL A CAT
STOLE IT AND
ATE IT.

ONE DAY
THE CARELESS FARMER
FORGOT MIKE'S
THROAT HOLE CLEARER
AT THE FAIR
AND
MIRACLE MIKE DIED
CHOKING ON
A KERNEL OF CORN
AT THEIR PHOENIX MOTEL.

JANIS JOPLIN DIED THE SAME WAY EXACTLY 46 YEARS AND 5 MONTHS LATER, LESS THAN 372 MILES AWAY.

GOOGLE IT.

oogle "Janis Joplin" & "Miracle Mike"

Web   Images   Videos   Shopping

About 1,720 results (0.48 seconds)

ARE
YOU
FEELING
SORRY
FOR
ROOSTERS
NOW?
THINKING
MAYBE
THEY
ARE
NOT
SO
BAD?

THIS
NEXT
STORY
WILL
PROBABLY
CHANGE
YOUR
MIND.

STOP
BEING
SO POSITIVE

A HEN WAS TRAVELING SLOWLY DOWN DUVAL STREET IN KEY WEST, FLORIDA.

A SLOW MOVING
SUV WAS TRAVELING
DOWN DUVAL STREET
AT THE SAME TIME.

UNFORTUNATELY, THE CHICKEN WAS MOVING SLOWER THAN THE SUV.

AND SHE WAS CRUSHED BENEATH THE MEAN TIRE.

A ROOSTER EMERGED FROM HIS STOMPING GROUNDS AT A NEARBY BAR AND RAN TOWARDS THE DYING HEN.

THE HUMANS
WITH BAD TIMING
WHO WITNESSED
THE HIT AND RUN
ASSUMED IT WAS
A GRIEF-STRICKEN
ROOSTER-HUSBAND
RUSHING TO
HIS DYING HEN-WIFE
AND THEIR BLACK HEARTS
FILLED WITH A GLINT OF
COMPASSION.

BUT THE ROOSTER
DID NOT RUN
TO THE DYING HEN
TO HELP OR TO MOURN OR TO
GIVE HER ONE LAST PECK ON
THE BEAK BEFORE SHE DIED.
HE CAME TO
HAVE SEX WITH
THE ALMOST-DEAD HEN.
AND THAT IS
EXACTLY WHAT HE DID.

AND
WHEN HE FINISHED,
HE STEPPED AWAY AND
CROWED AS IF TO
BRAG TO THE WORLD
ABOUT HIS
DIRTY DEED.

AND THEN
HE TURNED AROUND
TO GO BACK
FOR A SECOND ROUND
OF COCKERAL-NECROPHILIA.

BUT A RIVAL ROOSTER
HAD ALREADY APPEARED
ON THE SCENE
AND WAS HAVING HIS WAY
WITH THE POOR DEAD HEN.

**OF COURSE,
THE TWO STARTED
FIGHTING OVER
WHICH ONE GOT
TO MATE WITH
THE DEAD HEN
FIRST.**

AND THE HUMANS
WALKED AWAY
BROKEN, WONDERING
HOW THEY WOULD
EVER GET THAT IMAGE
OUT OF THEIR HEADS,
AND CONTEMPLATING
WHAT THEY SHOULD
DO NOW THAT THEY
DIDNT FEEL LIKE
EATING LUNCH
EVER AGAIN.

THE MORAL OF THIS STORY?

ROOSTERS
ARE ASSHOLES.

IT IS TRUE.

BUT IT SHOULD BE POINTED OUT THAT ROOSTERS THINK HUMANS ARE ASSHOLES TOO.

99

AND THEY ARE PROBABLY RIGHT.

HERE IS
A PHOTO OF
A PANDA BEAR
TO GET THAT IMAGE
OF ROOSTERS HAVING
SEX WITH A HEN
THAT WAS JUST
KILLED BY AN SUV
OUT OF
YOUR HEAD.

ROBONEAL.com

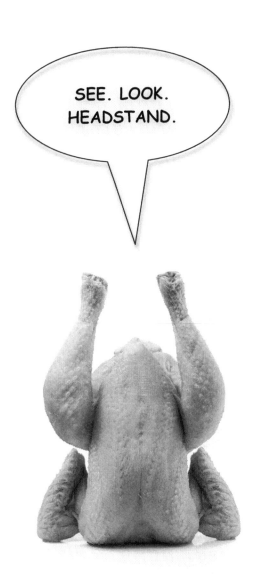

ABOUT THE AUTHOR

David L. Sloan is a begrudging bird enthusiast. He lives in Key West, Florida with anywhere from 6 to 36 chickens roaming around his fucking yard. Sloan has a blue and gold macaw named TJ who is expected to outlive him. Sloan used to tour as a chicken hypnotist on the carnival circuit, performing as Chicken Dave & The Traveling Rooster Show.

Made in the USA
Charleston, SC
18 May 2016